The Last Generation?

Shrinking Futures and the Global Fertility Crisis

GRB

Table of Contents

Introduction

Take a moment to notice the world around you. It may seem unchanged, but a quiet revolution is underway beneath the surface. Families have fewer children, classrooms are less crowded, and entire societies are slowly aging. This movement is happening all around us, but few have stopped to consider what it means. How will this new reality shape our future, our communities, and our children's lives? The question isn't whether the world is changing—it's whether we're ready to face the impact. In just half a century, the global fertility rate has plummeted from nearly five births per woman to just above two, with projections suggesting it may continue to decline; this dramatic change carries unprecedented implications (Bhattacharjee, 2021). Take a moment to digest that statistic. What does this mean for your family's future? How will these changes affect your community, your thoughts on parenthood, and the very fabric of society itself? Whether you're a parent planning for your children's futures, a researcher exploring socio-economic trends, or a concerned citizen reflecting on your role in this evolving world, you need to understand these trends.

Recently, as I watched my niece blow out the flickering candles atop her cake, surrounded by the warmth of friends and family, a wave of nostalgia washed over me, taking me back to my own childhood. The laughter that once filled our home with the chatter of siblings, cousins, and neighbors feels a world away, replaced by quieter times and smaller get-togethers. Is this change changing the essence of family—mine, yours, and everyone else's? Furthermore, how do these changes echo through the very walls of our homes, stretch across our communities, and send ripples that could reshape entire nations? In a world with fewer births, our greatest legacy will not be the numbers we produce but the sustainable future we create.

You might be wondering why any of this matters. How does a global drop in fertility rates affect you? This is not a distant demographic trend; it will affect every aspect of your life. From the economy and job markets to healthcare and retirement, the world around us will change in response to fewer children being born. Governments will need to rethink their policies, communities will need to adapt, and individuals like you will face new realities about how we live, work, and support one another. Our decisions today will determine whether this shift leads to a more sustainable and balanced world or one fraught with challenges. And that's why it matters—to all of us.

According to projections, one in six people will be 65 or older by 2050 (Bhattacharjee, 2021). Imagine a future where our parents and grandparents outnumber our children. What will that world look like? How will healthcare systems manage under the strain of increased demand? Economies are already grappling with these challenges—how will they adapt to shrinking workforces and the escalating need for elder care? What happens to the notion of the family when fewer children are born, and resources must be diverted to cater to the aging population? In the face of fewer births, we are tasked with a greater purpose: to nurture a planet where fewer people can live better, fuller lives.

We have to go deeper to fully comprehend the impact of this demographic shift. In the pages that follow, we will explore the myriad factors driving global fertility decline, from economic pressures and shifting cultural norms to advancements in reproductive health and education. We'll assess the health implications of low birth rates—not only for individuals or our own families but for society as a whole. While we will confront unpleasant truths, we will also spotlight innovative strategies worldwide designed to meet these challenges head-on. Declining fertility rates offer us a gift—a chance to reshape the future with more intention, responsibility, and hope for generations to come.

Moreover, we'll look at countries like Japan and South Korea, which are facing some of the lowest birth rates globally. Their experiences offer valuable lessons on the interplay between public policy and personal choices. On the other hand, we will explore regions like sub-Saharan Africa, where higher fertility rates persist, prompting us to consider various future projections and the potential balance of global demographics.

However, this book seeks to do more than simply present data and analysis. It will engage you—the reader—in a critical examination of the world we're shaping. What kind of future do you envision for your family and your community? What role can you play in aiming for sustainable change? You can influence demographic trends through the choices you make every day.

We'll also reflect on historical precedents to see how past societies navigated similar shifts. From the rise and fall of the Roman Empire to the post-World War II baby boom, history offers a rich range of lessons, revealing not only the challenges faced but also the resilience and adaptability of human societies.

Furthermore, we'll examine the broader sociocultural impacts of declining fertility rates. How will these shifts alter gender roles and the labor market? What changes are likely in educational priorities and social welfare programs? This affects you personally. What decisions can you make to improve your family's future? You'll see that demographic trends are closely linked to nearly every aspect of societal function.

Through compelling narratives about real people—families adapting to new realities, young adults rethinking parenthood, and elderly citizens finding their way in increasingly child-free environments—you'll connect with the statistics on a personal level, adding depth to our discussion.

We will also think about various future scenarios, envisioning how advancements in technology, such as artificial intelligence and robotics, might mitigate the impacts of a shrinking workforce. Could immigration play a role in addressing demographic imbalances between regions? Are there ways to encourage higher birth rates that respect your individual freedoms?

If you finish this journey, you'll understand global fertility shifts and your role in shaping the future. The demographic landscape is not beyond your influence—through informed conversations and thoughtful actions, you are empowered to help build a more balanced and sustainable world, prepared for the challenges ahead.

Keep in mind that the demographic landscape is constantly changing due to the collective actions and decisions of individuals, communities, and nations. As we navigate this tumultuous period of change, each of us plays a role in creating a balanced future prepared for the challenges ahead.

Imagine walking through a city where the majority of its inhabitants are over 60. Businesses cater to older generations, schools close their doors, and playgrounds remain empty. This may seem far-fetched, but in some parts of the world, it's already becoming a reality. These are the kinds of changes we'll explore in-depth—changes that are already underway but often go unnoticed.

Let's step boldly into the heart of demographic transformation and uncover what it truly means for you, your family, and our global society. As fertility rates decline, the world is evolving, and so too are the challenges and opportunities we face. The choices we make now will shape a more sustainable and balanced future for all. Now is your chance to help create a world where fewer means better.

References

Bhattacharjee, N. V., Schumacher, A. E., Aali, A., Abate, Y. H., Abbasgholizadeh, R., Abbasian, M., Abbasi-Kangevari, M., Abbastabar, H., Abd ElHafeez, S., Abd-Elsalam, S., Abdollahi, M., Abdollahifar, M.-A., Abdoun, M., Abdullahi, A., Abebe, M., Abebe, S. S., Abiodun, O., Abolhassani, H., Abolmaali, M., Abouzid, M., et al. (2024). Global fertility in 204 countries and territories, 1950–2021, with forecasts to 2100: A comprehensive demographic analysis for the Global Burden of Disease Study 2021. The Lancet, 403(10440), 2057-2099. https://doi.org/10.1016/S0140-6736(24)00550-6

CHAPTER 1
The Shift in Global Fertility Rates

The increase in human population was considered a sign of wealth and progress for millennia. However, the narrative is currently changing. The world's declining fertility rates are subtly rewriting the future of how societies function. What's causing this change? The reasons are numerous and varied, ranging from shifting social norms to shifting economic objectives. This is about more than simply fewer births; it's about completely changing economies, whole civilizations, and even the balance of power on Earth. We'll discover the underlying factors driving this demographic shift, and we'll explain why it matters now more than ever.

This chapter dives into the various aspects of this demographic shift, starting with an exploration of preindustrial fertility rates and societal norms that once favored large families. It then examines the transformative effects of industrialization and urbanization on family planning and structure. We'll analyze the post-World War II baby boom and subsequent declines in birth rates to show how the availability of availability and social movements have shaped reproductive decisions. On top of that, we'll talk about current global fertility trends, emphasizing the roles of education, economic stability, and urbanization. The chapter looks at these trends within the broader narrative of Generation Z, highlighting how past lessons inform their attitudes towards family life and reproduction. Ultimately, this analysis will give you a comprehensive understanding of the ongoing changes in global fertility dynamics and their significance for you, and for future generations.

Historical Overview of Fertility Rates

Historical contexts and socio-economic factors deeply rooted the decline in global fertility rates, necessitating an understanding of the trends that led to this significant shift (Nargund, 2009). By looking at preindustrial fertility rates and societal norms, the impact of industrialization on family planning, post-World War II baby boomers and their subsequent declines, and current global fertility trends, we can gain a lot of knowledge about the lessons learned from these transitions.

In preindustrial societies, fertility rates were notably high because of the lack of contraception and cultural norms that favored large families. Agrarian (agriculture-focused) economies thrived on the labor provided by children, who contributed significantly to the family's income and agricultural productivity. Cultural and religious beliefs often combined the need for large families with a high value on procreation. During this period, discussions around female autonomy and reproductive rights were virtually nonexistent since women's roles mostly came down to childbearing and homemaking. The high fertility rates of preindustrial societies have left an indelible mark on the gender dynamics and reproductive policies that have evolved over time.

The beginning of industrialization brought along dramatic changes in family planning and structure. People moved from rural areas to the cities in search of better economic opportunities, transforming the traditional family unit. Urbanization meant smaller family sizes because living in cities made it more difficult to raise large numbers of children. Nuclear families became more common, and the economic roles within these families began to change. With men increasingly working in factories and women taking on different roles within the household or even outside employment, the dynamics of parenthood and family size became different. This period marked the beginning of a broader acceptance of limiting family size and opened conversations about the responsibilities and financial implications of raising children in urban environments.

The post-World War II era saw a temporary spike in birth rates, known as the baby boom. Societies worldwide experienced a resurgence in births as soldiers returned home, and economies rebounded from the war's devastation. However, the 1960s saw a notable decline in fertility rates following this boom. The introduction and widespread availability of contraceptive methods played an important role in this reduction. In addition to this, the social revolutions of the 1960s and 1970s, particularly the women's liberation movement, heightened the emphasis on individual choice and autonomy regarding reproduction. The period also saw significant changes in societal attitudes towards family life, further influenced by shifts in economic stability and education. These changes laid the groundwork for modern views on fertility and family planning.

Today, global fertility trends continue to show remarkable variation across different regions and cultures. Current data shows a trend toward lower fertility rates, particularly in more developed nations where access to education and economic stability is higher. For instance, countries like Japan and Germany report some of the lowest fertility rates, while regions like Sub-Saharan Africa still have relatively high birth rates. Education, especially for women, is a critical factor influencing these trends. Higher levels of education correlate strongly with delayed childbirth and smaller family size, indicating that as more women pursue education and careers, fertility rates tend to decrease.

Economic stability is another important factor shaping global fertility trends. In places where economic conditions are stable and predictable, people feel more secure in making long-term plans, including family planning decisions. Conversely, in areas that are economically unstable, the uncertainty and financial strain often lead to delayed or reduced childbirth. These economic considerations highlight the interconnected nature of fertility rates with broader socio-economic conditions.

Understanding these trends places Gen Z within a larger narrative of historical demographic shifts. Gen Z, having grown up with unprecedented access to information and technology, is more aware of global issues, including population dynamics. They are also entering adulthood during a period of significant economic and social change, which influences their attitudes towards family life and reproduction. The rise and fall of fertility rates throughout history are not mere statistics—they are a mirror reflecting the evolving landscape of human society, culture, and aspirations. As this generation navigates their future, they carry forward the lessons learned from past demographic changes, continuing the dialogue on the balance between personal autonomy, economic realities, and societal expectations.

Impact of Urbanization on Fertility

The cyclical influence of modern society on fertility and the urban problems that come from it is a complex phenomenon that continues to reshape global demographics. One of the most significant contributors to this change is the move from rural to urban living. Cities have unique economic pressures that often compel individuals to prioritize their careers over family expansion. Historically, rural areas offered strong traditional support networks where extended families played a vital role in child-rearing. In contrast, urban environments tend to fragment these networks, making childcare more challenging and expensive. This disruption leads many young adults, particularly those from Gen Z, to postpone marriage and childbirth. The increased focus on career development in cities also aligns with the values that emphasize personal and professional growth, reflecting broader changes in society's priorities.

Access to education and employment for women has been another critical factor influencing fertility rates. Cities generally provide better educational and professional opportunities, allowing women to achieve higher levels of autonomy and financial independence. This empowerment often results in delayed childbirth, as women choose to invest time in their academic and career aspirations before starting a family. The correlation between female education and reduced fertility rates is well documented, highlighting a fundamental shift in demographic trends. Traditional perceptions of gender roles within the family undergo reevaluation as women increasingly participate in the workforce. For younger generations, including Gen Z, this shift represents a progressive move towards equality, but it also contributes to declining birth rates.

Housing and economic costs in urban areas further shape people's reproductive choices. The rising costs of living, including housing, healthcare, and education, significantly impact decisions regarding family size. Many people who live in cities opt for smaller families or decide against having children altogether to manage these expenses. The perception of economic instability associated with urban life can also stop people from pursuing larger families since financial security becomes a priority. Policymakers face the challenge of addressing these economic barriers to create sustainable urban environments that can support family growth. Without interventions that make urban living more affordable, the trend of declining fertility rates is likely to continue, worsening issues related to population aging and workforce shortages.

Cultural changes and evolving urban social norms also play an important role in shaping fertility patterns. These changes show up differently across various countries. For example, migration and tourism can alter population structures, leading to changes in fertility rates. Urban areas often have more progressive attitudes towards family planning and lifestyle choices, which can further contribute to lower birth rates. These cultural transformations affect not only fertility patterns but also the broader aspects of societal behavior and expectations.

The Implications of Urbanization for Future Generations

As birth rates decrease, aging populations increase, which creates potential challenges for maintaining a stable workforce and sustaining economic growth. Countries that have significant declines may face difficulties in supporting older generations, leading to increased pressure on social welfare systems. Beyond that, a shrinking youth demographic can mean less innovation and dynamism within the economy, which affects long-term prosperity and development.

Rapidly urbanizing nations like China provide a clear example of these dynamics. Rapid urbanization and the country's strict one-child policy have significantly reduced fertility rates. As a result, China now confronts the looming challenge of an aging population, with fewer young people available to support the elderly. This demographic imbalance threatens the country's economic stability and highlights the need for policies that encourage family growth while also addressing the economic pressures of urban living.

Similar trends exist in Western countries, albeit driven by different factors. Higher living costs in major cities, coupled with changing cultural attitudes towards family and work-life balance, have contributed to declining birth rates. For example, in cities like New York and London, the high cost of housing and childcare makes it difficult for many to consider large families. This economic reality forces young couples to delay or forgo having children entirely. As education and autonomy expand, the world's cradles grow silent—not from misfortune but from choice. The challenge of our era is balancing individual freedoms with the collective future of humanity.

What Should Be Done?

In order to empower people at the national and global levels to sustain population growth while maintaining autonomy, policymakers have to tackle these multifaceted challenges by creating environments that support families and promote balanced growth. Strategies could include implementing affordable housing initiatives, providing accessible childcare services, enhancing job security, and promoting flexible work arrangements to help parents balance their career and family responsibilities. Encouraging community-building efforts can also aid in reestablishing some of the traditional support networks that urban settings have lost, thereby facilitating the success of families.

To address the specific needs of women, policies should aim to expand access to quality education and equal employment opportunities while also providing support for balancing career and family life. Maternity and paternity leave policies, along with affordable childcare options, can empower both parents to share childcare responsibilities without sacrificing their professional goals. These measures not only benefit families but also contribute to a healthier, more resilient workforce.

Final Thoughts

The chapter's exploration of declining global fertility rates reveals the intricate interplay between historical contexts and socio-economic factors. From preindustrial society's high birth rates driven by labor needs and cultural norms to the transformative effects of industrialization on family size and structure, we see how changes in economic environments and societal attitudes have shaped reproductive trends. The post-World War II baby boom and subsequent decline highlight the critical role of contraception and social movements in empowering individual autonomy over reproductive decisions.

Today, the continued decline in fertility rates across various regions reflects broader socio-economic trends, like improved access to education and economic stability, particularly for women. Urbanization further complicates these dynamics by imposing financial pressures that often delay or reduce childbirth. As we consider the implications for future generations, it becomes clear that addressing these challenges requires comprehensive policy interventions. We can shape a future that fosters family life, balances societal needs, and achieves sustainable growth for future generations by learning from our past and adapting our policies.

References

Gu, D., Andreev, K., & Dupre, M. E. (2021, July 9). Major trends in population growth around the world. China CDC Weekly, 3(28), 604–613. https://doi.org/10.46234/ccdcw2021.160

Shead, S. (2021, December 7). Elon Musk says 'civilization is going to crumble' if people don't have more children. CNBC. https://www.cnbc.com/2021/12/07/elon-musk-civilization-will-crumble-if-we-dont-have-more-children.html

CHAPTER 2

What Low Fertility Rates Mean for Us

Each generation must discover its mission, fulfill it or betray it, in relative opacity.

–Frantz Fanon

Declining fertility rates are reshaping societies in profound ways. Low birth rates create changing age structures that influence not only the composition of populations but also the distribution of resources and responsibilities among different generations. As these shifts become more pronounced, we need to understand how they affect us all; from economic strains to healthcare pressures, the dwindling number of births is leading to a substantial increase in elderly citizens (Harris, 2006). This puts a lot of stress on systems that support aging individuals.

In this chapter, we will explore how declining fertility rates contribute to aging populations and heightened dependency ratios, which increase the burden on younger generations. We will discuss the economic ramifications of labor shortages, emphasizing the significant impact on critical industries such as healthcare and technology. Furthermore, we will delve into the potential intergenerational conflicts resulting from shifts in demographic priorities and explore the sustainable policy measures necessary to uphold economic stability and social security. This comprehensive analysis aims to give you a clear understanding of the multifaceted challenges posed by low fertility rates and give you ideas about viable solutions for mitigating their long-term effects.

Aging Populations and Dependency Ratios

As the cradle empties and the elder's chair fills, society faces a new dawn where the vitality of the young must balance the wisdom of the old. Low fertility rates are reshaping the demographic landscape profoundly. The phenomenon of low birth rates, typically described by fertility theories, alters the population structure, leading to a higher proportion of elderly citizens (Gemmill and Hartnett, 2020).

Fertility theories provide us with a framework to understand how low birth rates impact the age distribution within a population (Namboodiri & Wei, 1998). Essentially, when fewer children are born, the average age of the population increases (Cartwright, 2024). This leads to an aging population where the proportion of elderly citizens surpasses that of young people.

Understanding the dependency ratio, which represents the balance between working-age individuals and those who are dependent, such as children and the elderly, is crucial for understanding these changes. As fertility rates decline, the number of elderly dependents increases relative to the working-age population (Yenilmez, 2015). This imbalance puts more pressure on resources, particularly in terms of social services and healthcare.

The growing elderly population also needs more extensive care, which intensifies demands on the healthcare system. Age-related conditions like dementia, arthritis, and cardiovascular diseases become more prevalent (Salignon et al., 2023). This means that we need a robust and sustainable healthcare model to manage these issues effectively (Atella et al., 2019). Gen Z, the youngest segment of the current workforce, will increasingly bear the responsibility of addressing this demand. Their contributions are vital in creating innovative solutions that ensure the healthcare system can meet the needs of an aging population. Gen Z's ability to innovate and care, not only for themselves but also for a world where an aging population demands their support and ingenuity, is crucial for the future.

Intergenerational Challenges

> *Man sacrifices his health in order to make money. Then he sacrifices money to recuperate his health.*
>
> **—Dalai Lama**

Intergenerational challenges also come from this demographic shift. With a shrinking working-age population and a growing number of retirees, there is potential for conflicts in policy priorities. For example, older generations may prioritize pension and healthcare funding, while younger generations might want to focus on issues like education and employment opportunities (Knickman & Snell, 2002). Tensions can arise from this clash in priorities, necessitating a careful balance to meet the needs of both groups (Quadagno, 1989). When the fabric of society stretches between a growing elderly population and a shrinking youth, the true test lies in weaving a story that holds all generations together.

Social security systems, in particular, have to adjust to accommodate the changing population structure (Galasso, 2004). With fewer workers contributing to these systems and more retirees drawing benefits, there is a risk of financial strain. Policymakers need to explore sustainable approaches to ensure that social security remains solvent. This could involve rethinking benefit formulas, increasing retirement ages, or encouraging higher levels of workforce participation among older adults (Burtless & Quinn, 2000).

Gen Z will inevitably face the economic strain that comes from supporting an aging population. As they enter the workforce, they will encounter higher tax burdens and increased social service contributions that are required to fund pensions and healthcare for the elderly (Asmoro & Aini, 2022). This generation's willingness to engage in these responsibilities is important for maintaining societal stability and well-being (Machova, Seben & Kutna, 2019).

Resources shifting toward elder care can impact educational and career opportunities for Gen Z, too (Seemiller & Grace, 2017). Healthcare and social services catering to the elderly might receive investments traditionally earmarked for education and job training. This could limit the scope of opportunities available to younger people, potentially widening generational divides.

As healthcare costs rise because of the growing prevalence of age-related conditions, the economic burden on the younger generation will also become more intense (Schumacher et al., 2024). Addressing this challenge means we need innovative healthcare solutions and sustainable models that are capable of adapting to evolving demographic needs. Emphasizing preventive care and healthy aging initiatives can help mitigate some of these pressures so that the elderly maintain better health and independence for longer periods.

Gen Z can make significant contributions to the health workforce as future professionals (Dragolea et al., 2023). By pursuing careers in healthcare, they can help bridge the gap between the demand for medical services and the supply of qualified personnel. Encouraging young people to enter fields like nursing, gerontology, and primary care is necessary for preparing for the increasing healthcare demands of an aging population.

Economic Consequences: Labor Shortages

The economic ramifications of dwindling fertility rates present a multifaceted challenge, impacting labor markets, economic growth, and future generations. One primary consequence is the immediate workforce gap in critical sectors like healthcare, technology, and services. These industries are the foundation of societal well-being and economic stability. When there aren't enough qualified workers to fill these roles, productivity suffers. When fewer hands join the labor force, the engines of the global economy will slow, challenging growth and the well-being of future generations.

In technology, a lack of skilled labor can slow innovation and delay the development of new products and services that drive economic progress. Similarly, in the service sector, workforce shortages can lead to reduced business hours or service availability, inconveniencing consumers and decreasing overall economic activity. These effects show just how immediate and tangible the impacts of labor shortages can be on daily life and economic vitality.

A declining workforce also has a significant impact on the broader economy. A smaller labor pool directly affects Gross Domestic Product (GDP) growth rates (Date & Shimizutani, 2014). GDP growth relies on both the number of workers and their productivity. With fewer people entering the workforce, the potential for economic expansion is lower. This reduction can lead to economic contractions, particularly if sectors like manufacturing and agriculture can't get enough labor to maintain their production levels. In developed nations, where economic models depend heavily on continuous growth, this downturn can make fiscal challenges worse (Kearney & Levine, 2022), leading to higher public debt and a reduced capacity for public investment in infrastructure and social services. Empty workplaces, where the demand for skilled workers exceeds supply, represent the silent consequence of low fertility, threatening our collective prosperity.

Addressing Labor Shortages

Countries need to rethink how they acquire talent to address labor shortages. Outsourcing and international recruitment have emerged as immediate solutions. By tapping into the global talent pool, countries can fill gaps in their labor markets more quickly than waiting for domestic population growth to rebound. For example, many Western countries have increasingly relied on recruiting healthcare workers from abroad to meet demand. However, these practices also present challenges, such as ensuring the adequate integration of foreign workers into the workforce and society.

While outsourcing and international recruitment can offer short-term relief, they do not address the root cause of the problem: declining fertility rates. Therefore, long-term solutions require policy-driven approaches. Incentives for families to increase birth rates, like financial support for child-rearing, extended parental leave, and affordable childcare, are all fundamental measures. These policies aim to make it easier for families to have children and care for them, thereby gradually increasing the population over time.

Work-life balance policies are equally important. Modern work environments often place a lot of pressure on individuals, making it challenging to balance job responsibilities with family life. Offering flexible working hours, remote work options, and supportive workplace cultures can help parents remain in the workforce while raising children. Ensuring that workplaces are family-friendly not only supports current employees but also makes the prospect of starting a family more appealing to younger generations.

Moreover, technological advancements can play a role in mitigating some of the dependency pressures. Automation and artificial intelligence (AI) have the potential to compensate for lost labor by performing routine and even complex tasks efficiently. For instance, in manufacturing, robotic systems can take on repetitive tasks, freeing human workers to focus on roles requiring problem-solving and creativity. In the service sector, AI chatbots and automated customer service systems can handle basic inquiries, allowing human staff to concentrate on more nuanced customer interactions.

However, relying solely on technology is not a panacea. It is important to ensure that the existing and future workforce is prepared to work alongside emerging technologies. Educational systems need to adapt to these changes by offering training programs focusing on digital literacy, technological proficiency, and other relevant skills. Gen Z, in particular, will need to navigate an increasingly competitive job market that demands unique skill sets. Reskilling and upskilling opportunities for young people are vital to meet these evolving demands. Programs that provide technical training, coding boot camps, and certifications in high-demand fields can also help bridge these skill gaps.

Additionally, it's necessary to build a culture of lifelong learning. Encouraging continuous education and professional development allows workers to stay relevant and adaptable in a rapidly changing job market. Governments, educational institutions, and private companies all have roles to play in promoting and supporting lifelong learning initiatives.

Final Thoughts

We are all impacted by declining fertility rates, which profoundly alter our society. As more people enter their senior years and fewer babies are born, the balance tips toward an aging population. This shift places significant pressure on social services, healthcare systems, and the economy. For younger generations, this often means higher taxes and greater financial responsibilities to support a growing number of elderly citizens. You might already be feeling the impact through increased deductions on your paycheck or noticing strains on public resources.

This demographic change also brings about intergenerational challenges. Different age groups have varying needs and priorities—seniors may focus on pensions and healthcare, while younger people might prioritize education funding and job opportunities. Policy conflicts can arise from these differences, necessitating thoughtful solutions to ensure an equitable meeting of everyone's needs.

Economically, low fertility rates lead to labor shortages in crucial sectors like healthcare, technology, and services—the very fields that keep our daily lives running smoothly (Kohler, Billari, & Ortega, 2006). Fewer workers mean reduced productivity, slower economic growth, and limited innovation, which can affect everything from the availability of medical care to the development of new technologies that enhance our lives.

Short-term fixes like outsourcing work or hiring internationally can help fill immediate gaps but aren't sustainable solutions. What does this mean for you? It highlights the importance of policies encouraging higher birth rates and supporting families—like affordable childcare, flexible work arrangements, and parental leave (Kohler et al., 2006). Embracing new technologies, learning new skills, and being open to lifelong education will also be essential. These steps help adapt to demographic changes and pave the way for a resilient economy that benefits everyone.

By understanding these challenges and actively participating in the solutions, we can work towards a future where societal well-being and economic stability are ideals and realities we all share. It's about creating a world where both the young and the old can thrive—ensuring that our generation and those that follow have the opportunities and support needed for a fulfilling life.

Each generation holds the pen to humanity's next chapter; low fertility rates may leave those pages unwritten or leave blanks in many aspects of what we construe as development and progress.

References

Asmoro, P. S., Aini, E. K., & Nurlaily, F. (2022). Tax policy and financial access: Implications for entrepreneurial intention and entrepreneurial behavior among Generation Z. *Jurnal Akuntansi dan Keuangan, 24*(2), 57-67. https://doi.org/10.1234/jak.2022.24.2.57

Atella, V., Piano Mortari, A., Kopinska, J., Belotti, F., Lapi, F., Cricelli, C., & Fontana, L. (2019). Trends in age-related disease burden and healthcare utilization. *Aging Cell, 18*(1), e12861. https://doi.org/10.1111/acel.12861

Burtless, G., & Quinn, J. F. (2000). Retirement trends and policies to encourage work among older Americans. *Working Papers in Economics*, 175. https://doi.org/10.2139/ssrn.258078

Cartwright, A. (2024). *How many children?* Taylor & Francis.

Dragolea, L., Butnaru, G. I., Kot, S., Zamfir, C. G., Nuţă, A.-C., Nuţă, F.-M., Cristea, D. S., & Ştefănică, M. (2023). Determining factors in shaping the sustainable behavior of the Generation Z consumer. *Frontiers in Environmental Science, 11*, 1096183. https://doi.org/10.3389/fenvs.2023.1096183

Fanon, F. (n.d.) *Franz Fanon quotes.* Goodreads. https://www.goodreads.com/quotes/63103-each-generation-must-out-of-relative-obscurity-discover-its-mission

Galasso, V., & Profeta, P. (2004). Lessons for an ageing society: The political sustainability of social security systems. *Economic Policy, 19*(38), 64-115. https://doi.org/10.1111/j.1468-0327.2004.00128.x

Gemmill, A., & Hartnett, C. S. (2020, May 28). *Demographic drivers of the post-recessionary fertility decline and the future of U.S. fertility.* SocArXiv Papers. https://doi.org/10.31235/osf.io/2u78x

Harris, F. R. (Ed.). (2006). *The baby bust: Who will do the work? Who will pay the taxes?* Rowman & Littlefield.

Kearney, M. S., & Levine, P. (2022, January 9). The causes and consequences of declining US fertility. *Economic Strategy Group.* https://www.economicstrategygroup.org/publication/kearney_levine/

Kohler, H.-P., Billari, F. C., & Ortega, J. A. (2006). Low fertility in Europe: Causes, implications and policy options. In F. R. Harris (Ed.), *The baby bust: Who will do the work? Who will pay the taxes?* (pp. 48-109). Rowman & Littlefield.

Knickman, J. R., & Snell, E. K. (2002). The 2030 problem: Caring for aging baby boomers. *Health Services Research, 37*(4), 849-884. https://doi.org/10.1111/1475-6773.00169

Salignon, J., Rizzuto, D., Calderûh-Larraòaga, A., Zucchelli, A., Fratiglioni, L., Riedel, C. G., & Vetrano, D. l. (2022). What is an aging-related disease? An epidemiological perspective. *The Journals of Gerontology: Series A, 77*(11), 2168-2174. https://doi.org/10.1093/gerona/glac186

Machova, R., Seben, Z., & Kutna, A. (2019). Generation Z and Y versus tax literacy in the 21st century. *Journal of Applied Economic Sciences, 14*(2), 433-439. https://doi.org/10.14505/jaes.v14.2(58).06

Namboodiri, K., & Wei, L. (1998). Fertility theories and their implications regarding how low can low fertility be. *Genus, 54*(1/2), 37-55. Università degli Studi di Roma "La Sapienza".

Quadagno, J. (1989). Generational equity and the politics of the welfare state. *Politics & Society, 17*(3), 353-376. https://doi.org/10.1177/0032329289017003002

Seemiller, C., & Grace, M. (2017). Generation Z: Educating and engaging the next generation of students. *About Campus, 22*(3), 21-26. https://doi.org/10.1002/abc.21245

Schumacher, A. E., Aali, A., Abate, Y. H., Abbasgholizadeh, R., Abbasian, M., Abbasi-Kangevari, M., Abbastabar, H., Abd ElHafeez, S., Abd-Elsalam, S., Abdollahi, M., & Abdollahifar, M. A. (2024). Global fertility in 204 countries and territories, 1950–2021, with forecasts to 2100: A comprehensive demographic analysis for the Global Burden of Disease Study 2021. *The Lancet*. https://doi.org/10.1016/S0140-6736(24)00550-6

Yenilmez, I. M. (2015). Economic and social consequences of population aging: The dilemmas and opportunities in the twenty-first century. *Applied Research in Quality of Life, 10*(4), 735-752. https://doi.org/10.1007/s11482-015-9409-2

CHAPTER 3

Pro-Natalist Policies and Their Health Implications

> *It takes a village to raise a child.*

—African Proverb

As populations shrink and age, societies face a stark reality: without more families, the future of economic stability and social welfare hangs in the balance. But can policy alone inspire a generation to build the future? The answer lies in understanding the profound impact of supporting families in a world where every birth counts.

Pronatalist policies significantly impact public health and family well-being, affecting countries differently based on their unique socio-economic landscapes (Stone, 2020). These policies aim to encourage higher birth rates in various ways, like financial incentives, childcare support, and changes to family planning regulations (Demeny, 1986). By dissecting how individual nations have implemented pro-natalist strategies, we can learn more about both the successes and challenges that arise when prioritizing population growth.

In this chapter, we will consider two case studies from China and France to understand the direct and indirect outcomes of pro-natalist policies. We will look into China's experience with reversing its One-Child Policy and France's comprehensive family support system. Through these examples, you will get a thorough understanding of how different approaches to boosting fertility rates can shape public health and family dynamics.

China: The Reversal of the One-Child Policy

China is an example for the world where family size was defined by the One-Child Policy, which shaped the very fabric of daily life for several generations. This policy (Chinese: 孩政策; pinyin: yī hái zhèngcè) was a population planning initiative in China implemented in 1979 and lasted for 36 years to curb the country's population growth by restricting many families to a single child.

However, in a thoughtful and momentous shift, China revised this policy in 2015, opening the door to two children per family in response to the pressing needs of an aging population, a shrinking workforce, and the goal of sustainable growth. This change carries profound implications for Chinese society. To fully appreciate the impact of this policy shift, we must explore its intricate effects on family life, healthcare, and the country's long-term vision, understanding how this adaptation represents both a strategic and compassionate response to the needs of a changing society.

One major outcome of this policy shift is the change in family planning regulations. The One-Child Policy led to various social and economic repercussions (Jiang, 2024). On the other hand, projections suggest that China's universal two-child policy will have a limited impact on the nation's population growth, reaching a maximum of 1.45 billion by 2029. This policy will enable nearly all Chinese citizens to have the number of children they desire, decrease the number of abortions, eliminate unregistered children, and enhance health outcomes (Zeng & Hesketh, 2016).

However, as more families opt to have a second child, healthcare providers face heightened pressures, particularly in maternal and infant care (Li et al., 2019). This increase in birth rates can lead to potential overcrowding in hospitals and clinics, overwhelming the existing maternal and infant healthcare infrastructure.

Further, while some welcome the opportunity to expand their families, others remain cautious because of economic concerns and the pressures of modern life (Zheng, 2016). By 2050, despite the two-child policy, the proportion of elderly citizens will still surpass 26%, with the growing need for support from a shrinking workforce (Li, Zhou, & Jia, 2019). The country will see a slight increase in the younger population—about 5 million more births over the next few decades, but this increase, accounting for just 0.4% of total births by 2050, only slightly alleviates the pressures of an aging society (Li et al., 2019).

In urban areas, where living costs are high, many couples may still choose to have only one child or none at all, prioritizing financial stability and quality of life over larger family sizes. If women desire no more than one child and already have one, their intention to have a second child reflects low fertility autonomy. Research indicates that women who have less marital power than their husbands are more likely to desire a second child due to increased fertility pressure from their husbands (Qian & Jin, 2024). The results indicate that in post-reform urban China, escalating gender inequalities in labor markets are likely diminishing women's marital power. On the other hand, rural areas might see a more positive reception to the policy change, with cultural values often favoring larger families.

Long-term health considerations also play an important role in understanding the broader implications of the policy shift. China's aging population and restrictive two-child policy are placing significant pressure on its healthcare system, leading to increasing expenses related to chronic disease management and long-term care (Zhang, 2024). It is essential to enhance infrastructure, emphasize preventive care, and develop innovative solutions to ensure the resilience of the healthcare system. Programs aimed at providing nutritional support, regular health check-ups, and education can contribute to better health outcomes and overall family well-being.

France: Comprehensive Family Support Systems

Having examined the challenges and outcomes of China's policy reversal, we turn to France's proactive approach to supporting families through comprehensive policies that have yielded positive results in boosting fertility rates (Join-Lambert, 2016).

Nations that have these strong support policies generally exhibit higher fertility rates, and studies indicate that as family policies become more generous, fertility often increases. Theoretical models suggest that minimizing the expenses associated with raising children increases individuals' inclination to have children. Policies that assist parents in balancing work and childcare thus reducing opportunity costs, play a significant role in promoting higher fertility rates. Furthermore, increased participation of fathers in child-rearing can alleviate these costs, potentially enhancing fertility preferences, especially among mothers (Bergsvik, Fauske, & Hart, 2021).

One of the most significant factors contributing to France's success in raising birth rates is its robust system of family benefits. These benefits include direct financial subsidies, tax breaks, and allowances for families with children. By alleviating the financial pressures associated with raising children, these policies have made it more economically feasible. For example, the French government provides a monthly allowance for each child, which increases with the number of children in a family. This financial support reduces the economic burden on parents, encouraging them to expand their families without the fear of financial instability. The impact of these subsidies is evident in France's relatively high fertility rate compared to other European countries.

The influence of social class on the likelihood of having a second child reveals intriguing dynamics, demonstrating that although there are minor differences between household and individual viewpoints, a consistent trend is evident: women in higher social classes are more inclined to have a second child (Baizan, 2021). While there may be slight variations, couples generally share similar social standings, although women's class is typically a bit lower. Notably, women who are more inclined to have a higher number of children often have lower class attainment, and conversely, those with higher social standing tend to have fewer children. After considering selection effects, a clear positive relationship between social class and the probability of having a second child emerges, indicating that class remains a significant factor in family expansion decisions.

In addition to financial benefits, France's universal healthcare system plays an important role in supporting family health. Access to comprehensive reproductive health services ensures that all mothers receive necessary prenatal and postnatal care (Or et al., 2023). This universal coverage includes medical consultations, hospital stays, and maternal leave, which are necessary for both maternal and infant health. For example, French mothers benefit from paid maternity leave and job protection, allowing them to recover and bond with their newborns without the stress of losing their employment. This holistic approach to healthcare not only improves health outcomes for mothers and infants but also creates a sense of security among families (Beaujouan, 2020), making the decision to have more children less difficult.

In addition to the financial and healthcare support, France's social attitudes towards parenting foster a positive view of having children. In many French communities, there exists a cultural norm that emphasizes the importance of family life and collective responsibility for child-rearing. Programs like state-sponsored daycare centers and after-school activities help ease the burden on working parents, thereby encouraging larger families. This strong societal network not only supports parents logistically but also creates a sense of communal unity.

In France, beliefs about ideal parenting—characterized by attentiveness, patience, and emotional expressiveness—are in harmony with a cultural context that prioritizes strong family ties and child-focused parenting. These beliefs contribute to France's relatively high fertility rates compared to other European nations, where pro-natalist policies promote family growth by offering financial incentives, generous parental leave, and readily available childcare (Lin et al., 2023). This connection between cultural beliefs regarding ideal parenting and government support highlights how France's policies not only promote population growth but also reinforce values that parents find crucial for child-rearing.

The long-term impacts of these supportive family policies extend beyond immediate health outcomes, positively influencing demographic sustainability. For example, children raised in environments with strong social support and financial stability tend to have better health outcomes and educational achievements, contributing to a healthier future workforce. Furthermore, sustained population growth helps mitigate the adverse effects of an aging population by ensuring a balanced age demographic, which is vital for the continuity of social systems like pensions and healthcare.

Final Thoughts

Pronatalist policies have far-reaching implications for nations facing declining fertility rates, influencing everything from economic stability to societal structure. Effective pro-natalist measures, such as France's alignment of supportive family policies with cultural values of family care, can help sustain workforce levels, mitigate aging population pressures, and maintain balanced dependency ratios.

However, as seen in China, where policy adjustments alone have had limited effects on fertility, pro-natalist policies must resonate with deeper cultural and socio-economic factors to be effective. When pro-natalist policies fail to align with societal values or address economic barriers, their impact remains limited.

Efforts to encourage population growth must consider the diverse needs of families and the capacity of public health infrastructure. China's experience demonstrates the importance of upgrading healthcare resources to meet rising demands, while France's success showcases the benefits of integrated support systems for both parents and children.

References

Baizan, P. (2021). Welfare regime patterns in the social class-fertility relationship: Second births in Austria, France, Norway, and the United Kingdom. *Research in Social Stratification and Mobility, 73*, 100611. https://doi.org/10.1016/j.rssm.2021.100611

Beaujouan, E. (2020). Latest-late fertility? Decline and resurgence of late parenthood across the low-fertility countries. *Population and Development Review, 46*(2), 219–247. https://doi.org/10.1111/padr.12340

Bergsvik, J., Fauske, A., & Hart, R. K. (2021). Can policies stall the fertility fall? A systematic review of the (quasi-)experimental literature. *Population and Development Review, 47*(4), 913–964. https://doi.org/10.1111/padr.12455

Demeny, P. (1986). Pronatalist policies in low-fertility countries: Patterns, performance, and prospects. *Population and Development Review, 12*, 335–358. Wiley.

Jiang, J. (2024, August 18). China's one-child policy hangover: Scarred women dismiss Beijing's pro-birth agenda. *CNN.* https://edition.cnn.com/2024/08/18/china/china-one-child-policy-hangover-intl-hnk/index.html

Join-Lambert, H. (2016). Parental involvement and multi-agency support services for high-need families in France. *Social Policy and Society, 15*(2), 317–329. https://doi.org/10.1017/S1474746415000706

Li, H. T., Xue, M., Hellerstein, S., Cai, Y., Gao, Y., Zhang, Y., Qiao, J., Blustein, J., & Liu, J. M. (2019). Association of China's universal two-child policy with changes in births and birth-related health factors: National, descriptive comparative study. *BMJ, 366*, l4682. https://doi.org/10.1136/bmj.l4682

Li, H., Zhou, T., & Jia, C. (2019). The influence of the universal two-child policy on China's future population and ageing. *Journal of Population Research, 36*, 183–203. https://doi.org/10.1007/s12546-019-09223-3

Lin, G. X., Mikolajczak, M., Keller, H., Akgun, E., Arikan, G., Aunola, K., Barham, E., Besson, E., Blanchard, M. A., Boujut, E., & Brianda, M. E. (2023). Parenting culture(s): Ideal-parent beliefs across 37 countries. *Journal of Cross-Cultural Psychology, 54*(1), 4–24. https://doi.org/10.1177/00220221221087799

Or, Z., GandrÈ, C., Seppänen, A. V., Hernández-Quevedo, C., Webb, E., Michel, M., & Chevreul, K. (2023). *France: Health system review*. World Health Organization, Regional Office for Europe. https://doi.org/10.5203/9789289057483

Qian, Y., & Jin, Y. (2024). Women's fertility autonomy in urban China: The role of couple dynamics under the universal two-child policy. In *Fertility and childcare in East Asia* (pp. 195–225). Routledge.

Reupert, A., Straussner, S. L., Weimand, B., & Maybery, D. (2022). It takes a village to raise a child: Understanding and expanding the concept of the "village." *Frontiers in Public Health, 10*, 756066. https://doi.org/10.3389/fpubh.2022.756066

Stone, L. (2020). Pro-natal policies work, but they come with a hefty price tag. *Institute for Family Studies*. https://ifstudies.org/blog/pro-natal-policies-work-but-they-come-with-a-hefty-price-tag

Zeng, Y., & Hesketh, T. (2016). The effects of China's universal two-child policy. *The Lancet, 388*(10054), 1930–1938. https://doi.org/10.1016/S0140-6736(16)01379-0

Zhang, A. (2024). Adapting to demographic shifts: China's policy approaches in mitigating healthcare and retirement challenges posed by aging populations. *Journal of Education, Humanities and Social Sciences, 29*, 435–441. https://doi.org/10.1016/j.ehss.2024.04.012

Zheng, B. (2016). Population ageing and the impacts of the universal two-child policy on China's socio-economy. *Economic and Political Studies, 4*(4), 434–453. https://doi.org/10.1080/20954816.2016.1244099

CHAPTER 4

Way Forward—Future-Oriented Strategies

> *The future belongs to those who give the next generation reason for hope.*

–Pierre Teilhard de Chardin

Exploring future-oriented strategies to address the population crisis is a pressing necessity for nations worldwide (Nargund, 2009). As societies evolve, so must our approaches to building growth and maintaining a balanced age structure within populations. This chapter goes into various strategies designed to mitigate the population crisis. You'll find discussions on immigration as a vital tool to counteract demographic decline and rejuvenate economies. Furthermore, the chapter covers the importance of promoting gender equality and work-life balance, showing how these factors influence family planning decisions and support increased fertility rates.

The chapter further underscores the necessity of effective integration programs and comprehensive support systems that promote social cohesion. Through policy recommendations and real-life examples, we demonstrate how innovative and proactive strategies can ensure a sustainable demographic future.

Immigration: A Pathway to Demographic Renewal

Migration is an expression of the human aspiration for dignity, safety, and a better future. It is part of the social fabric, part of our very make-up as a human family.

—Ban Ki-moon

As many developed countries grapple with issues related to a dwindling workforce and increased pressure on social safety nets, immigrants bring vitality to these economies (Espenshade, Bouvier, & Arthur, 1982). We need to understand the multifaceted benefits of immigration to create effective policies that ensure successful integration, leading to long-term demographic sustainability.

One of the primary ways immigrants contribute to economic growth is by filling labor shortages. Many sectors, including healthcare, technology, agriculture, and manufacturing, face significant challenges due to an insufficient native workforce. Immigrants often have the skills and willingness to work in these industries that have labor deficits (Aitken, 2022). Furthermore, immigration policies can greatly impact entrepreneurship by drawing in talent and boosting economic vitality

(Nazereno, Zhou, & You, 2019). Nonetheless, social networks and co-ethnic communities also influence relocation choices. These enterprises not only employ additional workers but also add innovation to the market.

Achieving successful integration necessitates tackling complex challenges such as identity negotiation, social cohesion, and resource accessibility—ensuring that immigrants can fully engage in society. The global experience of immigration underscores the importance of flexible policies that honor cultural heritage while encouraging inclusion and economic stability for a sustainable future (Clark, 2021). Successful integration programs are instrumental in maximizing the benefits of cultural enrichment. For example, language training and educational initiatives help immigrants adapt more quickly, allowing them to participate fully in the local economy and society. Local governments and community organizations play an important role in implementing such programs, ensuring newcomers feel supported (Stewart et al., 2008). Examining models from countries with robust integration programs can provide valuable insights. Programs that build on social harmony and mutual understanding include community engagement activities, mentorship schemes, and public awareness campaigns aimed at highlighting the positive contributions of immigrants (Pacquiao, 2018).

There is a need for a "new social contract" that prioritizes intergenerational cooperation and social cohesion. Immigration serves as an essential mechanism for maintaining economic stability by addressing workforce shortages and bolstering public services (Myers, 2007); however, effective integration and favorable public perception are vital for maximizing its advantages. To encourage mutual support among generations, the focus should be on the development of policies that are community-oriented. By embracing these strategies, nations can strive for a resilient future that values contributions from all age groups and cultural backgrounds, fostering both economic sustainability and social unity.

According to Thiel de Bocanegra et al. (2018), effective immigration policy must be evidence-based and designed to comprehensively and transparently address public concerns. Effective pathways for legal immigration should emphasize skills and economic needs while also addressing humanitarian concerns. Policies aimed at attracting skilled immigrants in high-demand sectors can help alleviate urgent labor shortages and foster innovation-driven growth. Moreover, establishing streamlined procedures for recognizing foreign qualifications and professional credentials facilitates the quicker integration of immigrants into the workforce.

To fully realize the potential of immigration as a remedy for demographic challenges, comprehensive support systems are vital for helping newcomers flourish and make meaningful contributions to their communities. These support measures encompass access to affordable housing, quality healthcare, and educational opportunities, all of which lay the groundwork for stability and growth (Stewart et al., 2008).

Pilot programs could test innovative immigration policies prioritizing family reunification and economic contribution. There are suggestions to implement a pilot program for an effective immigration system that acknowledges the hard work of immigrants, honors their families, and ensures economic advantages for both the citizens of the host country and the newcomers (Peri, 2012).

Straightforward, transparent, and fair rules that are easy to understand and consistently applied should form the foundation of such a system. Flexibility is essential to respond to evolving immigration trends and labor market needs. Acknowledging the complexities of comprehensive reform, a practical approach involves first tackling the most pressing failures of the current system—especially those that create unnecessary costs and obstacles. By implementing small, manageable changes, such as introducing temporary labor market visas, policymakers can showcase immediate benefits like enhanced efficiency, greater employer satisfaction, reduced incentives for unauthorized work, and increased government revenue. This incremental approach enables the system to gain momentum through economic success before addressing more contentious issues, ultimately laying the groundwork for comprehensive reform.

Promoting Gender Equality and Family-Friendly Policies

As former United Nations Secretary-General Kofi Annan wisely stated, "Gender equality is more than a goal in itself. It is a precondition for meeting the challenge of reducing poverty, promoting sustainable development, and building effective governance."

The feminization of global labor flows and the unique vulnerabilities experienced by migrants underscore the need for a more nuanced approach to the Sustainable Development Goals (SDGs). Policies and programs designed to achieve the 2030 Agenda must incorporate considerations of gender and migration for genuinely informed and effective outcomes (Holliday, Hennebry, & Gammage, 2019). Additionally, civil society and established human rights frameworks play a crucial role in ensuring a comprehensive and universal application of the SDGs, particularly for populations impacted by migration or displacement in their development rights.

Research shows that in countries where gender equality is emphasized, women feel more secure, both financially and personally, when making decisions about starting families (Holliday, Hennebry, & Gammage, 2019). For example, Scandinavian countries, known for their high gender equality indices, also report higher fertility rates compared to other developed nations.

Women are postponing motherhood for reasons like financial stability and finding suitable partners, but this often does not lead to parenthood. A study of childless women aged 25 to 40 showed that while some became parents, most continued to delay or decided against having children due to obstacles such as financial constraints or lack of partners (Niemistˆ et al., 2021). This trend may result in declining birth rates and changing family structures, impacting economic planning and social support systems.

To tackle the gender dynamics affecting careers and motherhood, organizations should implement fair hiring practices, support affordable childcare, and encourage shared domestic responsibilities. Enhancing access to reproductive healthcare and career development tailored to women's needs can help them balance professional and personal aspirations (Bonache et al., 2022). Integrating gender-sensitive considerations into migration policies is also fundamental. By creating an inclusive culture that values work-life balance and promotes gender equality, societies can empower individuals to fulfill their potential.

Furthermore, gender equality in the workplace creates an environment where women do not have to choose between their careers and families (Dowd, 1989). Workplaces can empower women by offering equal pay, removing gender biases, and ensuring opportunities for career advancement (Martin, 2021).

Organizations that provide flexible work arrangements, such as remote work options or adjustable schedules, help parents more effectively balance their professional and personal responsibilities. These arrangements foster a supportive environment where employees feel valued and acknowledged, promoting a culture that recognizes the significance of family life. Companies that emphasize work-life balance typically experience increased employee satisfaction and productivity, which in turn encourages employees to consider starting or growing their families.

Leading employers such as Audit Wales, Citigroup, Crown Prosecution Service, Grant Thornton, Imperial College London, NatWest Group, North East London NHS Foundation Trust, Pinsent Masons, Senedd Cymru/Welsh Parliament, and Yorkshire Building Society have enacted policies that support working families. These include flexible working arrangements, improved parental leave, childcare assistance, career development initiatives, and inclusive workplace cultures (Garg & Agrawal, 2020). Such policies not only benefit employees but also boost organizational performance, serving as exemplars of purposeful policy design and leadership aimed at addressing the gender dynamics influencing careers and parenthood, ultimately contributing to a more equitable society.

Family-friendly policies help reduce the pressures faced by modern families by creating a supportive environment. Companies like Google and Microsoft provide parental leave, childcare services, and flexible work options, enabling parents to care for their children without experiencing financial strain (Trask, 2017). These practices enhance job satisfaction, increase productivity, and lower turnover rates. Moreover, implementing family-friendly policies addresses broader societal challenges, such as declining birth rates and gender equality. For instance, companies like Patagonia illustrate how these practices promote social cohesion and community well-being. By prioritizing employee welfare, organizations can attract top talent and encourage sustainable demographic and societal growth (Garg & Agrawal, 2020).

Cultural Shifts, Education, and Engagement

We need societal changes to promote shared parental responsibilities and promote healthier family dynamics (Lidbeck & Bostr^m, 2019).

This involves promoting active participation from both mothers and fathers, challenging stereotypes, and normalizing fatherly involvement. Media campaigns and community initiatives can help dismantle stereotypes and bolster men's confidence in their parenting skills. Supportive policies and flexible workplace arrangements are equally important. Additionally, educational reforms and early interventions can shape attitudes from a young age, preparing future generations to adopt more equitable family models (Vachon & Vachon, 2010). Shared parenting benefits children, parents, and society by offering diverse perspectives and nurturing approaches.

Media campaigns play a significant role in reshaping societal perceptions of parenting. Advertisements and public service announcements that depict fathers actively participating in childcare can normalize this behavior and influence broader cultural shifts. When society views parenting as a shared responsibility, it reduces the stigma associated with men taking on nurturing roles, thus encouraging more balanced family dynamics (Lim, 2021).

Community initiatives that engage men in childcare are particularly effective. Programs that involve fathers in early childhood education or parenting workshops help break down stereotypes and build a more equitable approach to raising children. This shift not only supports family growth but also ensures that children benefit from the diverse perspectives and nurturing styles of both parents.

Increasing awareness about the importance of gender equality and work-life balance is a cornerstone of driving policy change. Educating young adults about the benefits of equitable gender roles and the significance of family-friendly policies can shape future generations' attitudes towards work and family life. Schools, colleges, and community centers should incorporate programs that challenge traditional gender norms and emphasize the value of shared responsibilities (Kuteesa, Akpuokwe, & Udeh, 2024).

Engaging policymakers, businesses, and educators in promoting gender equality initiatives is just as important. Policymakers can create frameworks that incentivize organizations to adopt family-friendly policies, while businesses can implement practices that support work-life balance. Educators can develop curricula that highlight the importance of equitable gender roles in achieving overall societal well-being (Levine et al., 2024).

Advocacy groups also play a big role in pushing for systematic changes that are conducive to family growth. These groups can lobby for legislative reforms, raise public awareness, and collaborate with various stakeholders to create a supportive environment for families. For example, advocacy groups in several countries have successfully campaigned for extended parental leave policies, resulting in positive outcomes for family growth.

Final Thoughts

Throughout this chapter, we have examined innovative strategies that address the population crisis by increasing fertility rates and promoting demographic sustainability. Immigration emerges as a necessary solution to counterbalance declining birth rates and aging populations. Countries can rejuvenate their economies and enrich their cultural landscapes by integrating immigrants into the workforce and society. Immigration can play a pivotal role in achieving long-term demographic stability and social harmony with effective policies and support systems.

In parallel, promoting gender equality and work-life balance is essential for encouraging family growth. Societies can create environments where individuals feel secure and supported in starting families by ensuring equal opportunities and implementing family-friendly policies. Cultural shifts that emphasize shared parenting responsibilities further strengthen these efforts. Through comprehensive approaches that include policy changes, community initiatives, and educational awareness, we can foster a sustainable demographic future that benefits all members of society.

References

Aitken, R. J. (2022). The changing tide of human fertility. *Human Reproduction, 37*(4), 629–638. https://doi.org/10.1093/humrep/deac020

Bonache, H., Carballo, V., Chas, A., & Delgado, N. (2022). Go the extra mile: A gender approach towards parenthood in early-career academics. *Journal of Gender Studies, 31*(1), 125–135. https://doi.org/10.1080/09589236.2021.1929402

Dowd, N. E. (1989). Work and family: The gender paradox and the limitations of discrimination analysis in restructuring the workplace. *Harvard Civil Rights-Civil Liberties Law Review, 24*, 79.

Espenshade, T. J., Bouvier, L. F., & Arthur, W. B. (1982). Immigration and the stable population model. *Demography, 19*(1), 125–133. https://doi.org/10.2307/2060970

Garg, S., & Agrawal, P. (2020). Family-friendly practices in the organization: A citation analysis. *International Journal of Sociology and Social Policy, 40*(7/8), 559–573. https://doi.org/10.1108/IJSSP-03-2020-0053

Holliday, J., Hennebry, J., & Gammage, S. (2019). Achieving the sustainable development goals: Surfacing the role for a gender analytic of migration. *Journal of Ethnic and Migration Studies, 45*(14), 2551–2565. https://doi.org/10.1080/1369183X.2018.1510064

Ki-Moon, B. (2013, October 3). *Secretary-General's remarks to High-Level Dialogue on International Migration and Development.* United Nations. https://www.un.org/sg/en/content/sg/statement/2013-10-03/secretary-generals-remarks-high-level-dialogue-international-migration-and-development

Kuteesa, K. N., Akpuokwe, C. U., & Udeh, C. A. (2024). Gender equity in education: Addressing challenges and promoting opportunities for social empowerment. *International Journal of Applied Research in Social Sciences, 6*(4), 631–641. https://doi.org/10.25125/ijarss.v6i4.7862

Levine, C. S., Bourne, K. A., Song, R., & Weltzien, K. (2024). Creating inclusive schools to reduce health and well-being disparities. *Social and Personality Psychology Compass, 18*(1), e12841. https://doi.org/10.1111/spc3.12841

Lidbeck, M., & Boström, P. K. (2021). "I believe it's important for kids to know they have two parents": Parents' experiences of equally shared parental leave in Sweden. *Journal of Social and Personal Relationships, 38*(1), 413–431. https://doi.org/10.1177/0265407520909565

Lim, A. (2021). Confucian masculinity: State advocacy of active fatherhood in Singapore. *Men and Masculinities, 24*(1), 46–63. https://doi.org/10.1177/1097184X20941853

Martin, L. J. (2021). Delaying, debating and declining motherhood. *Culture, Health & Sexuality, 23*(8), 1034–1049. https://doi.org/10.1080/13691058.2020.1840770

Myers, D. (2007). *Immigrants and boomers: Forging a new social contract for the future of America.* Russell Sage Foundation. https://www.russellsage.org/publications/immigrants-and-boomers

Nargund, G. (2009). Declining birth rate in developed countries: A radical policy re-think is required. *Facts, Views & Vision in ObGyn, 1*(3), 191–193. PMCID: PMC4255510.

Niemistˆ, C., Hearn, J., Kehn, C., & Tuori, A. (2021). Motherhood 2.0: Slow progress for career women and motherhood within the 'Finnish dream'. *Work, Employment and Society, 35*(4), 696–715. https://doi.org/10.1177/09500170211003740

Pacquiao, D. (2018). Culturally competent multicultural workforce. In *Global applications of culturally competent health care: Guidelines for practice* (275–286). Springer. https://doi.org/10.1007/978-3-319-45729-2_18

Peri, G. (2012). Rationalizing US immigration policy: Reforms for simplicity, fairness, and economic growth. *Brookings Report.* https://www.brookings.edu/research/rationalizing-us-immigration-policy-reforms-for-simplicity-fairness-and-economic-growth/

Stewart, M., Anderson, J., Beiser, M., Mwakarimba, E., Neufeld, A., Simich, L., & Spitzer, D. (2008). Multicultural meanings of social support among immigrants and refugees. *International Migration, 46*(3), 123–159. https://doi.org/10.1111/j.1468-2435.2008.00464.x

Theilhard de Chardin, P. (n.d.) *Pierre Theoilhard de Chardin quotes.* Goodreads. https://www.goodreads.com/author/quotes/5387.Pierre_Teilhard_de_Chardin

Thiel de Bocanegra, H., Carter-Pokras, O., Ingleby, J. D., Pottie, K., Tchangalova, N., Allen, S. I., Smith-Gagen, J., & Hidalgo, B. (2018). Addressing refugee health through evidence-based policies: A case study. *Annals of Epidemiology, 28*(6), 411–419. https://doi.org/10.1016/j.annepidem.2017.05.010

Trask, B. S. (2017). Alleviating the stress on working families: Promoting family-friendly workplace policies. *National Council on Family Relations Policy Brief, 2*(1), 1–6. https://www.ncfr.org/sites/default/files/2017-10/Policy-Brief-2-1.pdf

Vachon, M., & Vachon, A. (2010). *Equally shared parenting: Rewriting the rules for a new generation of parents.* Penguin.

CHAPTER 5

Summarizing the Global Demographic Transformation

The future depends on what we do in the present.

—Mahatma Gandhi

In this chapter, we look into the necessity of aligning policies with the evolving demographic landscape to create sustainable growth. The chapter highlights important elements and lays out comprehensive frameworks for international cooperation and community involvement. Through cohesive strategies and interdisciplinary collaboration, societies can adapt to demographic challenges, ensuring stability and progress. This chapter also provides guidance on building awareness and education, empowering you with knowledge, and encouraging collective action to safeguard the well-being of future generations.

Summarizing the Impact of Changes

Both we, as individual citizens and society at large, need to understand the causes and consequences of these changes to craft informed responses and strategies for sustainable futures.

Current fertility trends point to a noticeable decrease in birth rates globally. While some countries still maintain higher rates, many others face rapid declines, influenced by a range of socioeconomic factors. This variability creates a complex demographic patchwork that requires nuanced and region-specific policy interventions. For example, countries like Japan and Russia are grappling with declining populations, prompting measures aimed at encouraging larger families, whereas some African countries may encounter different challenges related to youthful populations. These contrasting scenarios highlight the need for tailored policy frameworks that address the unique demographic circumstances within each region.

A significant contributor to falling fertility rates is the impact of socioeconomic factors on individuals' life choices. Economic instability often leads to delayed parenthood. Additionally, societal transformations have seen increased emphasis on education and career development, particularly among women, who now pursue higher degrees and professional achievements before considering family life. This shift not only influences personal timelines but also intersects with broader demographic trends, as fewer children per family gradually reshape population structures. The interconnectedness of these socioeconomic dimensions with fertility rates underscores the importance of aligning economic and social policies to support family growth without compromising individual aspirations and economic stability.

These socioeconomic influences are putting increasing pressure on healthcare and social structures. Addressing these challenges involves rethinking healthcare delivery models to accommodate changing demographics, ensuring that systems can sustainably cater to an evolving population profile. Without these reforms, the risk remains that aging societies may face unsustainable burdens.

However, countries cannot operate in isolation; demographic shifts are transnational issues that necessitate coordinated international efforts. Global citizenship becomes important in forging multinational collaboration and ensuring policy coherence across borders. Initiatives that focus on cooperation among nations can lead to more effective responses to demographic changes, capitalizing on shared knowledge and resources. Constructing platforms for dialogue and partnership encourages innovation in addressing complex demographic challenges, enabling countries to draw from a collective pool of expertise and experience.

Guidelines for successful international cooperation involve promoting cultural sensitivity, respecting national sovereignty while embracing global perspectives, and building open channels of communication among involved parties. Establishing common goals and objectives can enhance cooperation, allowing for synergistic actions tailored to diverse regional contexts. By building robust frameworks for collaboration, the international community can better navigate demographic shifts and ensure sustainable progress.

Reflecting on these major trends affecting global fertility rates reveals their profound implications for future action. Understanding the interplay of contributing factors becomes fundamental in shaping informed policies and practices as declining birth rates transform societal landscapes. Proactive engagement with these dynamics prepares societies not only to adapt to current realities but also to anticipate future demographic developments. This thorough comprehension fosters resilience in communities, empowering stakeholders to implement strategic measures conducive to sustainable population growth.

Inspiring Action for an Inclusive Future

Community engagement plays a pivotal role in addressing fertility-related challenges. Local initiatives and grassroots movements serve as catalysts to increase demographic awareness, empowering citizens to actively participate in shaping future policies. In many communities, grassroots organizations work tirelessly to highlight the importance of demographic trends and mobilize action. They can organize community forums, workshops, and outreach programs that bring together diverse voices to discuss solutions and raise awareness about the benefits of addressing population decline. These efforts must involve youth, the torchbearers of tomorrow. By integrating young people into decision-making processes and equipping them with leadership roles within community initiatives, we nurture a generation that prioritizes sustainable demographic practices.

Education and awareness are central to understanding and acting upon demographic challenges. Incorporating demographic education into school curricula ensures that future generations are well-versed in the implications of fertility trends. Schools can offer courses focusing on sociology, demography, and economics, providing students with the tools to analyze and interpret demographic data critically. Public seminars and campaigns can also play a significant role in informing citizens about the ramifications of population decline. These platforms offer opportunities for experts to share insights, presenting data and case studies that show the interconnectedness of demographic changes with broader societal impacts. Additionally, educational institutions could partner with media outlets and technology providers to create engaging content that reaches a wide audience, ensuring that the messaging around demographics is both widespread and impactful.

Collaboration across sectors is important for developing innovative solutions to demographic challenges. Partnerships should span government, the private sector, and civil society to harness diverse perspectives and expertise. Governments can lead by creating inter-ministerial task forces that focus on demographic issues, ensuring that policies reflect a holistic understanding of societal needs. The private sector, meanwhile, can innovate by introducing products and services that address demographic shifts, like developing technologies for remote work or providing childcare solutions. Civil society organizations bring invaluable insights into community-specific challenges and can facilitate dialogue between different groups. For example, NGOs specializing in women's rights and health can provide useful feedback on reproductive health policies, ensuring they are effective and inclusive. Cross-sector collaboration also promotes sharing best practices, allowing stakeholders to learn from one another's successes and change strategies when needed.

Final Thoughts

Throughout this chapter, we have talked about the transformative shifts in global fertility rates and their extensive societal implications. Socioeconomic factors influence these demographic changes, which vary by region. For nations that have population decline, creating policies that encourage family growth is fundamental. Conversely, countries with youthful populations face different challenges that require distinct approaches. By understanding these dynamics, individuals and policymakers can develop strategies that are both regionally relevant and globally informed, ensuring a sustainable future.

To pave the way for a more inclusive tomorrow, it is necessary to take action based on the data discussed. Policies designed to bolster population growth have the potential to address these demographic challenges. Grassroots movements and educational initiatives play pivotal roles in raising awareness and promoting community engagement. Additionally, collaborative efforts between government, private sectors, and civil society can drive innovation and create solutions tailored to diverse needs.

References

Date, Y., & Shimizutani, S. (2014). Why has Japan's fertility rate declined?: An empirical literature survey with an emphasis on policy implications. *Japanese Economy, 34*(1), 4-45. https://doi.org/10.1080/10971434.2014.960191

Gandhi, M. (n.d.) *Mahatma Gandhi quotes*. Goodreads. https://www.goodreads.com/quotes/806111-the-future-depends-on-what-we-do-in-the-present

Conclusion

—Lao Tzu

In this exploration of population decline, we've walked through a landscape marked by numerous significant themes. Each chapter has aimed to expose the interconnected factors driving global fertility dynamics and their implications for society at large. We've talked about how economic development, urbanization, and women's empowerment have reshaped our demographic realities, forging new paths across diverse regions. Understanding these elements isn't merely an academic exercise; it's about framing the future that awaits us if these trends remain unchecked.

The urgency for action in response to declining fertility rates is not just a call to government officials or academics—it's an appeal to every reader who has gone through these pages. With the specter of labor shortages and an aging population hovering over many nations, the stakes are higher than ever. The scenarios we've examined make it clear that passive observation is no longer enough. We must implement proactive strategies today to mitigate these potential crises. This is not merely a demographic issue; it's a societal transformation crying out for immediate attention.

We can take heart from countries that have pioneered successful initiatives amidst similar challenges. Consider France, with its comprehensive family support systems that stand as a testament to how well-conceived policies can promote social well-being. Meanwhile, Singapore's financial incentives have offered valuable insights into encouraging higher birth rates without sacrificing quality of life. These stories of success not only serve as benchmarks but also remind us of what's possible when administrations commit to thoughtful, evidence-based approaches.

Yet, addressing the demographic shifts threatening our societies demands more than isolated efforts—it requires a collective drive, harnessing the strengths and perspectives from multiple sectors. Governments alone cannot shoulder the burden of creating effective solutions. Involving organizations with different expertise and community members who experience these changes firsthand ensures that the policies created will be both inclusive and sustainable. This spirit of collaboration is necessary if we are to construct a resilient framework capable of adapting to a range of complex issues associated with declining fertility rates.

As citizens, academics, policymakers, or merely concerned observers, there lies before us an opportunity—and indeed, a responsibility—to rethink how demographic decline shapes our families, communities, and countries. Recognizing the inherent interconnectedness of these themes allows us to better appreciate the broader picture, where each decision and policy impacts the next generation's world.

For those dedicated to research within this sphere, the critical insights drawn from this book provide a strong foundation for further inquiry. The various intersections of sociology, economics, and public health outlined herein offer a variety of avenues to explore innovative solutions and expand our comprehension of these fundamental issues. By continuing to build on the knowledge shared in these chapters, scholars can advance studies that fundamentally alter the way we perceive and address fertility trends.

Ultimately, none of this can happen in isolation. It requires a shared commitment to advocating for change and pushing past apathy into realms of meaningful action. Whether implementing policies at a governmental level or shifting societal attitudes towards family and work-life balance, every step taken contributes to remedying the imbalances posed by population decline.

Thus, as we conclude this discourse, let us embrace the challenge before us: to convert awareness into action and doubt into determination. By doing so, we set the stage not only for grappling with current issues but also for creating environments where future generations can thrive, harmonizing population growth with economic stability and social progress. Let this book be more than a record of demographic analysis;

let it be a catalyst for tangible, positive change that resonates within personal and national spheres alike.

Low fertility rates, if not addressed, can lead to a gradual global population decline, pushing some countries towards a demographic crisis. This situation results in an aging population, a shrinking workforce, and increased pressure on social support systems, potentially causing economic stagnation and diminishing cultural vitality. Without proactive measures like supportive prenatal policies and technological innovations, demographic imbalances may worsen, making it harder for families to have children due to limited childcare access, insufficient parental leave, and inadequate reproductive healthcare.

However, there are hopeful pathways forward. Policymakers and communities can create family-friendly environments by investing in comprehensive prenatal policies, offering financial incentives, and improving childcare accessibility. Embracing advancements in reproductive health technologies can also assist those facing infertility challenges. These efforts, combined with a cultural shift that values families, can help stabilize and reverse declining fertility trends. The conversation about the global fertility crisis is just beginning, with upcoming books that will provide deeper insight and solutions aimed at fostering a sustainable future for future generations.

We are currently at a critical juncture that necessitates deliberate decisions and cooperative endeavors. The course of action we choose will shape the destiny of our societies and influence how coming generations perceive their world. As readers equipped with newfound understanding, you hold the power to effect change, whether through informed debate, policy advocacy, or initiating grassroots movements that resonate on a larger scale.

Thank you for being part of this crucial conversation. It is with hope and confidence that we look forward to witnessing the transformative impact that arises when knowledge meets action, setting a progressive course toward demographic equilibrium that serves humanity's best interests. Let this conclusion be a starting point, a springboard for innovation, commitment, and ultimately, a brighter future for all.

Glossary

Aging Population: A demographic trend characterized by an increasing proportion of elderly individuals within a population, often due to declining birth rates.

Affordable Housing: Housing options that are economically accessible to a broader range of the population are crucial for family planning.

Advocacy Groups: Organizations that promote specific causes or interests, often working towards social justice, policy reforms, and the rights of marginalized populations.

Automation and AI: Technologies that perform tasks traditionally done by humans, which can help mitigate labor shortages by increasing efficiency in various sectors.

Childcare Regulations: Laws and policies governing the availability and quality of childcare services, which influence families' ability to balance work and parenting.

Collaborative Efforts: Joint activities and partnerships among various stakeholders, including government, private sector, and civil society, to tackle shared challenges.

Community Engagement Activities: Initiatives designed to involve community members in social efforts, fostering connections and support among different groups.

Contraceptive Methods: Techniques and devices used to prevent pregnancy.

Cohesive Strategies: Integrated approaches that unify various elements to create effective responses to complex challenges like declining birth rates.

Cultural Changes: Shifts in societal values and attitudes that can affect personal choices, including decisions about family size and parenting.

Cultural Heritage: The traditions, customs, and values that shape the identity of a community, influencing how immigrants are integrated into society.

Cultural Norms: Shared expectations and rules that guide the behavior of members of a particular society or group, including attitudes toward family and parenthood.

Cultural Sensitivity: Awareness and respect for cultural differences that affect interactions and relationships among individuals and groups in a diverse society.

Economic Consequences: The financial implications stemming from demographic shifts, including impacts on GDP, productivity, and public investment.

Economic Stability: A condition where economic performance is stable, characterized by balanced growth, low unemployment, and manageable inflation rates.

Educational Achievements: The extent of educational attainment and success, which can be influenced by family support systems and socio-economic factors.

Educational Initiatives: Programs and efforts aimed at improving knowledge and understanding of specific topics, such as demographic trends and fertility issues.

Educational Opportunities: Access to programs and resources that enhance learning and skill development are crucial for supporting immigrant integration and workforce readiness.

Entrepreneurship: The activity of creating new businesses or ventures, often enhanced by the skills and diverse perspectives that immigrants bring.

Family-Friendly Policies: Supportive measures implemented by organizations and governments to assist families, such as parental leave, childcare support, and flexible work arrangements.

Family Support Systems: Policies and services provided by the government or organizations to assist families, including financial aid, childcare, and healthcare services.

Fertility Preferences: Individuals' attitudes and desires regarding the number of children they wish to have are often shaped by socio-economic, cultural, and personal factors.

Fertility Rates: The average number of children born to a woman over her lifetime, influencing population age structure.

Fertility Trends: Patterns and changes in birth rates within a population over time, influenced by various socio-economic factors.

Financial Subsidies: Monetary support provided by governments to help cover costs related to raising children, which can encourage larger families.

Gender Equality: The state of equal access to resources and opportunities regardless of gender, which can influence family planning decisions and workforce participation.

Gender Inequality: The unequal treatment or perceptions of individuals based on their gender, which can impact family size decisions and women's autonomy in childbearing.

Grassroots Movements: Community-based initiatives led by local individuals or organizations that advocate for social change and awareness, often focusing on specific issues like population dynamics.

Healthcare Delivery Models: Systems and processes through which health services are provided to populations, which may need to be adapted to accommodate demographic changes.

Healthcare Infrastructure: The organizational framework, resources, and facilities needed to deliver healthcare services to a population.

Healthcare Pressures: Strains placed on healthcare systems due to a growing elderly population requiring more medical attention and age-related care.

Interdisciplinary Collaboration: Cooperative efforts that bring together experts from different fields to address complex issues, leveraging diverse perspectives and expertise.

Intergenerational Conflicts: Disagreements and tensions that arise between different age groups, especially regarding policy priorities and resource allocation.

Immigration: The process through which individuals move from one country to another to settle, often contributing to economic growth and addressing labor shortages in host countries.

Integration Programs: Initiatives aimed at assisting immigrants in adapting to their new country, including language training, education, and community engagement.

Labor Shortages: Situations where the demand for workers exceeds the supply, often impacting vital sectors such as healthcare and technology.

Lifelong Learning: The ongoing, voluntary, and self-motivated pursuit of knowledge for personal or professional development throughout an individual's life.

Long-Term Health Considerations: Factors related to the ongoing health needs of a population, particularly as it ages, which may influence public health policy and infrastructure development.

Maternal and Infant Care: Healthcare services focused on the health of mothers and babies during pregnancy, childbirth, and the postnatal period.

Maternity and Paternity Leave: Policies allowing parents to take time off work after the birth of a child, promoting family bonding and care.

Opportunity Costs: The potential loss of benefits that could be gained from alternative choices when resources (like time and money) are limited, impacting decisions on family size.

Population Crisis: A significant decline in birth rates leads to demographic imbalances, aging populations, and potential economic challenges for societies.

Population Growth: An increase in the number of individuals in a population, often influenced by birth rates, death rates, and migration.

Post-World War II Baby Boom: A significant increase in birth rates following World War II, driven by returning soldiers and economic recovery.

Preindustrial Societies: Communities that existed before the industrial revolution, typically characterized by high fertility rates and large families.

Pro-Natalist Policies: Government initiatives aimed at encouraging higher birth rates through various incentives and support systems.

Proactive Strategies: Anticipatory measures designed to address potential issues before they arise, especially in the context of population and demographic challenges.

Public Awareness Campaigns: Organized efforts to inform and educate the public on specific issues, aiming to influence opinions and encourage collective action.

Shared Parental Responsibilities: The collaborative involvement of both parents in child-rearing tasks aimed at promoting gender equality and family well-being.

Sociological Factors: Elements related to social behavior and structures that influence individuals' decisions and opportunities.

Societal Implications: The broader effects and consequences of demographic changes on social structures, economic development, and community dynamics.

Societal Norms: Accepted behaviors and practices within a society that influence people's choices and attitudes towards family and reproduction.

Social Cohesion: The bonds that unite members of society, promoting mutual support and collaboration across different cultural and age groups.

Social Contract: An implicit agreement among members of a society regarding their rights and responsibilities towards each other, particularly in terms of support for individuals and families.

Social Class Dynamics: The influence of one's social and economic class on decisions related to family size, child-rearing, and childbearing preferences.

Social Security Systems: Government programs designed to provide financial support to individuals in retirement or unable to work, which may face strain as demographics shift.

Skilled Labor: Workers who possess specialized knowledge or abilities that are essential for particular industries, often in high demand.

Sustainable Growth: Economic development that meets present needs without compromising the ability of future generations to meet their own needs, particularly in terms of population and resource management.

Sustainable Policy Measures: Strategies that aim to ensure economic stability and social security while adapting to demographic changes over time.

Two-Child Policy: A policy implemented in China in 2015 allowing families to have two children, aimed at addressing demographic challenges like an aging population.

Urbanization: The movement of people from rural areas to cities, often resulting in changes in lifestyle, economic opportunities, and family size.

Work-Life Balance: The equilibrium between work responsibilities and personal life, which can affect family planning and participation in the workforce.

Image References

Christina. (n.d.). *Two women sitting beside table and talking* [Image]. Unsplash. https://unsplash.com/photos/two-women-sitting-beside-table-and-talking-LQ1t-8Ms5PY

Gumerova, S. (n.d.). *Eiffel Tower, Paris across body of water during daytime* [Image]. Unsplash. https://unsplash.com/photos/eiffel-tower-paris-across-body-of-water-during-daytime-m-sVLnrjFxY

Holmes, M. (n.d.). *Shallow focus photography of woman carrying baby in front of house* [Image]. Unsplash. https://unsplash.com/photos/shallow-focus-photography-of-woman-c

Landkammer, H. (n.d.). *A woman and a child are walking on the beach* [Image]. Unsplash. https://unsplash.com/photos/a-woman-and-a-child-are-walking-on-the-beach-KvIZtJX1k4s

Lute. (n.d.). *A group of people standing in front of a large circular structure* [Image]. Unsplash. https://unsplash.com/photos/a-group-of-people-standing-in-front-of-a-large-circular-structure-CZH-Crxa_E4

Mossholder, T. (n.d.). *2 women walking on the road during daytime* [Image]. Unsplash. https://unsplash.com/photos/2-women-walking-on-the-road-during-daytime-FIdkkBWmF7Y

Papanastasopoulos, Y. (n.d.). *People walking on the street* [Image]. Unsplash. https://unsplash.com/photos/people-walking-on-the-street-whLWBRF1S2Y

Patel, R. (n.d.). *Bird's eye view of car on road* [Image]. Unsplash. https://unsplash.com/photos/birds-eye-view-of-car-on-road-4W5cp9vxLag

Sarah B (n.d.). *A man with glasses and a watch* [Image]. Unsplash. https://unsplash.com/photos/a-man-with-glasses-and-a-watch-fxjOz-GWC04

Sergeichik, O. (n.d.). *Shallow focus photography of baby beside woman* [Image]. Unsplash. https://unsplash.com/photos/shallow-focus-photography-of-baby-beside-woman-MrsbKzRzflo

Toochinda, T. (n.d.). *Girl holding purple and green camera toy* [Image]. Unsplash. https://unsplash.com/photos/girl-holding-purple-and-green-camera-toy-GagC07wVvck

Vas, A. (n.d.). *Man walking on road in front of building* [Image]. Unsplash. https://unsplash.com/photos/man-walking-on-road-in-front-of-building-vBSZXCiNNd0